CLASSIC BIBLE STORIES
THE LIFE OF CHRIST

retold by Lise Caldwell
with art from the Standard Publishing Bible art collection

© 1998 The Standard Publishing Company, Cincinnati, Ohio.
A division of Standex International Corporation. Printed in U.S.A.
Library of Congress Catalog Card No. 97-50563
Graphic design and layout by Coleen Davis and Dale Meyers

Christ Is Born

Luke 2

When it was almost time for baby Jesus to be born, Mary and Joseph left Nazareth and went to Bethlehem, as Caesar had ordered.

When they got to Bethlehem there was no room for them in the inn, so they slept in a place where the animals were kept. Baby Jesus was born in there. Mary wrapped the baby in strips of cloth to keep him warm and laid him in a manger to sleep. Mary and Joseph thanked God for the baby Jesus.

Shepherds who were out in the fields saw an angel in the sky. The angel told them about the baby born in Bethlehem. Then angels filled the sky, praising God. The shepherds hurried to see the child. Afterward, they told everyone in Bethlehem about the angel's message.

JESUS IN THE TEMPLE
Luke 2

When Jesus was twelve years old, he went with his parents to Jerusalem to celebrate Passover. After the feast was over, Mary and Joseph began the journey home. Many people were with them on the road to Nazareth. Soon Mary and Joseph realized that Jesus was not with them. They went back to Jerusalem and found him in the temple sitting with the teachers. He was listening to them and asking them questions. They were all amazed by how much he understood about God. His mother asked him, "Why didn't you come with us? We have been looking for you for three days!" Jesus answered, "Didn't you know that I was in my Father's house?" Mary and Joseph did not understand him, but they knew he was special. They all went back to Nazareth. And Jesus continued growing wise and strong, obeying Mary and Joseph and pleasing God.

The Baptism of Jesus

Matthew 3, Mark 1, Luke 3

Jesus came from Galilee and went to the Jordan River to be baptized by his cousin John. But John said, "I should not baptize you! You should baptize me."

But Jesus said, "Baptize me now. It is right." So John baptized Jesus in the Jordan River. When Jesus came out of the water, the Spirit of God came down like a dove and landed on him. He heard a voice from heaven which said, "This is my Son. I am very pleased with him."

After this Jesus went to the desert. Satan came and tempted him three times, but Jesus did not do anything wrong. Then angels came and took care of him.

Jesus Heals a Man Who Cannot Walk

Mark 2, Luke 5

Four men took their friend who could not walk to Jesus. They wanted Jesus to make him walk.

When they got to the house where Jesus was teaching, it was so crowded they could not get their friend inside. So they cut a big hole in the roof. Carefully the four men lowered the mat their friend was lying on right down in front of Jesus.

Jesus said to the man, "You are forgiven for the wrong things you have done. Stand up and walk." The man stood up, picked up his mat and walked out the door.

The people who saw this were amazed. They knew that Jesus must be special to forgive a man for his sins and make him walk again.

Jesus Feeds More Than 5,000 People

Matthew 14, Mark 6, Luke 9, John 6

One day Jesus taught a crowd of people all day long. The people began to get hungry, but there was no where for them to buy food.

Jesus asked Philip where the disciples would find food to feed them. Philip said that it would take almost a year to pay for enough food to feed so many people.

Andrew, Peter's brother, said, "Here is a boy with five loaves of bread and two small fish." Jesus had the people sit down. There were about 5,000 men among them, along with women and children.

Jesus thanked God for the boy's lunch. He told his disciples to give it to the people. There was enough for everyone! In fact, there were twelve baskets full of leftovers!

Jesus Calms a Storm
Matthew 8, Mark 4, Luke 8

Jesus had been teaching crowds of people all day. The crowd was so big that he got into a boat with his disciples and taught from there. After he was finished teaching he and his disciples took the boat further out into the water.

While Jesus and his followers were in the middle of the lake, a terrible storm came. Jesus' followers were scared, but Jesus was asleep in the stern of the boat. The disciples woke him up. "Help us! We are going to drown!" they shouted.

Jesus got up and said to the water, "Quiet! Be still!" Immediately the roaring wind was silent and the crashing waves stopped. The lake was calm. Jesus' followers were amazed. "Even the wind and waves obey Jesus," they said.

Jesus Enters Jerusalem

Matthew 21, Mark 11, Luke 19, John 12

Jesus and his followers were coming near Jerusalem for Passover. Jesus sent two of his followers into a town, telling them, "You will find a donkey tied there with her colt. Untie them both and bring them to me." The followers did what Jesus told them to do. They threw their coats over the colt and Jesus rode on him.

People from Jerusalem were excited about him coming and ran out to meet him. Some threw their coats on the road in front of him. Some waved palm branches. They shouted, "Hosanna! Praise God! God bless the One who comes in the name of the Lord. Praise to God in Heaven." The crowd praised Jesus as he entered Jerusalem.

The Lord's Supper

Matthew 26, Mark 14, Luke 22

Jesus and his twelve disciples ate the Passover meal together in a large upper room. While they ate, Jesus said that one of them would betray him. He knew it would be Judas.

Jesus thanked God for the bread, broke it, and said to his disciples, "Eat this. This is my body that is given for all of you. Whenever you eat this, remember me."

He took wine and thanked God for it, and said to them, "This is my blood which will be shed for many people. I will not drink any more wine until I drink it in the kingdom of God."

Some of the disciples argued about which one of them was the most important. Jesus said, "Do not be like the world, with slaves and masters. Instead, the most important of you should behave like a servant, just as I am a servant."

Jesus Prays in the Garden

Matthew 26, Mark 14, Luke 22

After Jesus and his disciples had finished eating the Passover meal, they all went to the Mount of Olives, where they had been many times before.

When they got there they went to a garden in a place called Gethsemane. Jesus asked Peter, James, and John to walk with him. They could see that he was very sad. He asked them to pray.

He walked a little farther and knelt down and prayed, "Father, if it is possible, do not let me drink from the cup of suffering. But do not do what I want, do what you want." Then he went back to Peter, James, and John. They had fallen asleep.

Jesus woke them up and told them to pray so that they would be strong against temptation. Two more times he went to pray, and two more times he came back and found them asleep. The third time he told them to get up, because Judas had brought the soldiers to arrest him.

Jesus Is Crucified
Matthew 27, Mark 15, Luke 23, John 19

Jesus was nailed to a cross on a hill called Golgotha. Two thieves were crucified with him, one on each side. The Roman soldiers made a sign that said "The King of the Jews" and nailed it above his head. The people made fun of him. "He saved other people. Why can't he save himself?" they asked.

Jesus asked his Father to forgive all the people who hurt him. "They do not know what they are doing," he said.

That afternoon he died on the cross. When he died, the earth shook and rocks split. The curtain of the temple was torn in half from top to bottom.

The men guarding him saw what happened and said, "Surely this is the Son of God!"

The Resurrection

Matthew 28, Mark 16, Luke 24, John 20

Jesus' body was put in a tomb owned by Joseph of Arimathea. The next day was the Sabbath. When the Sabbath was over, Mary Magdalene, Mary the mother of James, and Salome went to the tomb to put spices and perfume on Jesus' body. On their way to the tomb, they wondered who would roll the heavy stone away that blocked the entrance to the tomb.

When they got there, the stone had already been rolled away. When they went inside the tomb, a man dressed in white said, "You are looking for Jesus who was crucified, but he is not here. He is risen! Tell his disciples to go to Galilee—they will see him there."

Soon all the disciples heard the news. Jesus was not in the tomb! He had risen!

Look for these other products featuring Standard's Classic Bible art collection:

Classic Bible Stories, A Family Treasury (03848)

Classic Bible Stories, The Old Testament (04257)

Classic Bible Stories, The Old Testament: Coloring Book (22045)

Classic Bible Stories, The Life of Christ: Coloring Book (22046)

Classic Bible Stories, A Reproducible Coloring Book (02255)

12 Classic Bible Art Teaching Pictures: Old Testament (02290)

12 Classic Bible Art Teaching Pictures: Life of Christ (02289)